Scarcely Carry
All Vast Woods

Also by Peter Larkin

Enclosures
Prose Woods
Pastoral Advert
Terrain Seed Scarcity
Slights Agreeing Trees
Sprout Near Severing Close
Rings Resting The Circuit
What the Surfaces Enclave of Wang Wei
Leaves of Field *
Lessways Least Scarce Among *
Imparkments (The Surrogate Has Settled)
Give Forest Its Next Portent *
City Trappings (Housing Heath or Wood)
Introgression Latewood *
Trees Before Abstinent Ground *
Encroach to Resume *
If Trees Allay an Earth Retrialling *

Wordsworth and Coleridge: Promising Losses

* *Titles from Shearsman Books*

Peter Larkin

Scarcely Carry All Vast Woods

Shearsman Books

First published in the United Kingdom in 2025 by
Shearsman Books
PO Box 4239
Swindon
SN3 9FN

Shearsman Books Ltd Registered Office
30–31 St. James Place, Mangotsfield, Bristol BS16 9JB
(this address not for correspondence)

EU AUTHORISED REPRESENTATIVE:
Lightning Source France
1 Av. Johannes Gutenberg, 78310 Maurepas, France
Email: compliance@lightningsource.fr

www.shearsman.com

ISBN 978-1-84861-973-9

ACKNOWLEDGEMENTS

My title is a quotation from 'Extinction Songs' (2024) by Jonathan Skinner, itself derived from Gaucelm Faidit, used with permission and many thanks. Grateful thanks to these magazines and their editors where extracts from some of these poems first appeared: *Fortnightly Review, International Times, Junction Box, Shearsman, Stride, Tears in the Fence.*

My greatest debt as ever is to Tony Frazer and Shearsman Books for enabling this collection to appear.

Contents

For Jonathan Skinner and for Stephen Collis

Engladings (Englynion)

1

Never a settled stance at enhancing unless the hills petition:
after preaching sedentary green to the island
greener thirst of any chance-pliant plant

2

Tree to a lunge is how an element switches ground,
swatches (of lean-to) have been to
the conicals of its swaddling the rebound

3

Soils, why so green-come, took colours off steep winter?
Long haunches, time grows a petulant green
over pale yewtrees, a transform hunch-steady

4

Discrete horizons press on concrete continua, not thrown over, just
an unspilt at being so given over,
ocean feathering the off-flutter of land

5

Brave tackle very rod, shapely bidden, well-hidden in shrift:
spindle and juniper chariots of natural act,
how prayer is upcast pith and arm

6

Tempo as topology glides tuitions or advisory entrussments *onto* space,
reckoning the durational undertow of middle things,
how an unremoved bough creates new attributes

7

Does present a towards of the sampled, examples para-representative:
forwarding assent is tall secondary miracle,
perforated stare of leaf agency simple adjacency

8

Landscape its whole crescent slice of beseech, one beech each:
or at times by a token oak,
its rarest foil so nearly above holly

9

Tree-grapple any assault is accustomed to bring: despite place
wish that some cording fleck its tag,
scarce then but not serried in arrears

10

Lets conceal what resigns bare to the chest of seed,
the stewarding will foster many muffled alerts,
in proportions of shallows where it dabbles

11

As spun off should be neighbours, rare to the full:
winds sweep offbelt the sack thickening woods,
bespeaks a carrier not gone upon expedition

12

Remission at the nape of branch, defray contention: hazel adjudges
it suspensive (new attentions) of the conflict,
dispense bracken and broom from general turnout

13

Notables of the stood, common tree (accessioning) oils the bowl,
smooths a final sprawl of woodland shafts,
retire spike and enrol ancient horny trees

14

Compressive braces in tree-cutting, ivied hazel the only hospital,
atones in immature commotion, as evasive undergrowth
will sound immune ringing of parted forest

15

Freest of all counter-slippages from removal, penalty of lopping
is these targeted limbs, larger reversionary adhesions
scarce as every risen distraught series was

16

Ripe fruit safeguards bushes, whose palisade is juice converting raid.
Alder ahead of lime, piecing its firsts,
ivy pure respite in seeking an appearance

17

Tree toward passage inclines every cancelled sheath of its return:
one drift in midst (sift) of leaves,
surges and dormancies, for purges and normalcies

18

Operative stasis not oasis but full standing at relational take:
here settled (adjacently whittled) as believe periderm
receives it, pouch of tree announce implication

19

Linkage heeds branched texture, foliage fetched, a rift in a
rib in raft of receiving, low-pressure
emphatics, at local crook its own unsawn

20

Pilot of the shaded decoy, limbed from hill to hill,
along the stoppages (spiral strappage brief mending)
of a wood which ridges bail out

21

Green waves freshly cut (float) where a flood is due,
diving then the scan of imbued horizons,
prompts a coast for shore of oak

22

Woods a without of effort, woods a within of effect,
that safe core rinds before it climbs,
cavities of thicket hollow in field density

23

Congealed branching wounds in one, thorns those are my palms:
over-stretching woods congregate green-teamed, as
much abroad as any grievance of shelter

24

Diagonal hands rear a branch-time's durational escapement, locally collapses
infolds cut from the delay of it,
what outswing curtails for a covered slope

25

Less post-reductive originals but a scarcer conduct of gift,
every common rarity each such sponsored horizon,
prayer in slender depth result sprung from

26

A tree's uncanny sketch of its prehistory, the central rebate:
offshoots provoke need-points preseeding their want:
prayer reminds periphery to hold itself spare,
not here the living disuse of recuperation

27

Woody crown a force-field of gift, itself a *recess*
in creation, pods, blains, recentre the undersheet,
the litter from what cranes at root

28

Trees will scold lift, any measure of it, a green
swerve (to staff) scorns much less, serves
a reach more than their own revision

29

Tree-spore confiding in cleft, poverty no longer a suspension
too provisional for linking, what sinks alive
into attachments ahead: emboldened outrig *as* enfolded

30

Weary the meshing but full sheen in crashes of light:
what exact peck at a latticed complexion
crystalises and awards, retaliates but dis-hoards

31

A pale stack signifies transferable lack, a lesser continuity missing
its nothing, beside pressure of acute respite,
prolific life abridged to its sessional community

32

Depends (amended) on leaf textures grown to the offer-of
what is not spun but dispositional: not
full reskirting, wholly engrossed, gently received, afeared

33

A thud of care, no mere dribble at the world:
if the outline does demarcate, it growls
at expensive offcuts, prays its self-brandishing

34

A wad of reefed clips, a scrunch of tree, announces
(atones) the implication, whose beddings
are not the same amplification, semi-clad

35

Spasms by which to take on the laden, at the
crook of an uncrannied oak: an edge-
of-field betook it, this medial prism

36

Trouble-prongs (probes, props) of pasture roving over knuckles for
limbs, patches of livid other-strife, crabbed
vivid at a retrieval's rich poked interval

37

Green gradient prod of leaf, its silver under-shirt, imparts
a clotting of root to a differential
weather of seasonal appetite by shaken shoot

38

Assistant (appellant) discords their acute unprivilege in the swell to
leaf: discards are ancillary, not alternative relief:
a prime offerable ample on leanest greenbridge

39

Trees not quite now the slenderer consequent of an arm:
any antimony of belonging declares the embrace,
plays the analogue of a prior day

40

Paradox of prayer in a self-organising (auto-browsing) universe:
field of fields now arena on call,
a woodland receiver ramifies (rezones) the despoil

41

To flatten out the forest is to mislead its folds.
swivelled horizontals it bowed to, floors horizons
at half-play, a brinkless world away

42

A tree's trade is to be shipped to its own
seclusion, no other refusal than leaf plunging
(waking) leaf, each avoidance another surgent refuge

Note

These poems are very loosely derived from the Welsh *englyn penfyr*, traditionally involving a stanza of 3 lines, the first with 10 syllables, the second with 5-6 and the third with 7. I have, more basically and less fleetly, substituted a word-count for the syllabics and forgot the second line was intended to be at least one syllable shorter, so my pattern is a line of 10 words followed by two of seven. One poem goes for a fourth line.

Some of the contributory material is filtered through translations provided by Francesco Benozzi in his excellent *Landscape Perception in Early Celtic Literature* (2004).

The Contusion Has No Rind

Note: This poem is dedicated to the terrain west of Berkswell (Warwickshire) and especially Sixteen-Acre Wood where HS2 has been gouging its way beside and across.

What was once aligned larching knows a new unapparent lunge———
mechanic plantation plunges into new exception to give adjacent
acceleration its need——rindless lineation

A harsh treed space at the diminution———interruption of two
impositions, one at the rate of rinds of growth, the other the applied
abstraction of bolting a landscape to its dread shots

Trees over the edge of get a setting———to sow my leaf a seed that
can't be outspread on earth———an only access pitch thrust beyond
its entrances———in the wake of its own compliance, hedged brittly
awake

Firming a persistent second strand of lineation which this plantation
already was———now snapped out at its wired green continuances

Wrecked the inter-denominational threads of cross-scape———webs
that don't allow a next plane such immediate access

Not next encroaching but nearer encoaching———a trajectory prime
thrust without residue, not even a contrary strewing this near———
cued to this gear

If plantations disforested this ground, can't now recall rails to any other
amendment, amoundment———here clearance is not even its own
new cutting———alien alignments less any foray———unbestowed
upstream influence

Torn by an unaffordable refuge, to be an innovatory bystander not born
of any peripheral recognition———fresh imperturbables will race past
its blank (green) windows———soft median ingrown trees, curtailed
from any windward coarsening———speed shutters for the worsening

Silently exhumed in a stark preparative for noise———the impact will have already vanished before its exactly naked absorbance———trees with such directional intentions sheerly (scarcely) accoutred

Can anything bear down lightly on future (upright) reeds of scope, a layup for the self-arrival of green sticks?———a sheen of interfoliage, invitations everywhere, to be a presage less any traversal?

To stand knowing, trip-bestowing, amid a litter of acquainted trees ———quartered against their own thriving, not yet reduced enough to bury this their counter-spurn

A purposed scrape over ground-moss, congealed leaves, occasions of passage ferried minus warp (curl) onto universal directness———global levels of acceleration rapid enough for body but not avid enough for breath

A ground-smack only initial?———what purport for surfaces of the new rindlessness?———pactive transmission has no other wrinkle ———the new accelerative peace of running on our elsewheres, lineside suspension of contrition———hyper-retention of the incision, any associate statics strict invisibles

Every tree implicated in contrary abatement, dead-end carriage of their own hacked passage———accounts of injected leeway no longer need to expound———any rebound only as rigidly perishable as the trees

Deceptions of high-speed corridor can only be stationary, provincial, interruptibles of blinked consequence———a shafted plantation is put to flight in its outlay incidence

Exact single shift now deprived of other frugal consistencies, of pleading for rind where clotting is a located refreshment———a horniness which binds ligament to ligament in a semi-flexed (seasonal) landscape

A railway's strictures too far, surplus immediate attainment———solely a rind's is local content, foreshortened, pleated not contused——— unsaturated but a sated skin, not infused or smoothed abroad

Between spokes at speed amid spikes of a fixed tide———the whole contrast as such totters toward tertiary flexing and niching———global distances sue for some local additive

Given the plantation can't hide, can only slide past its altered demarcation, distortions that no longer proffer to tremble at the root——retreat dissembles and disanoints———or at the horizon of some recession in the disassociation

Latent marginality at its fierce gleaning———transdisposition of neighbourhood———the bias of a hill dashed onto a plate, either flank is concentric platform

Incompatible linkages, a mask for the entire landscape, one supreme inter-disruption——— obsolete hinter-instructions, ante-exception

A train of synchronisations added by line on line, former names missing their patchwork———speed pure fretwork, the set-forward of any location surpassed

Ascribe our landscape to the length of our universe, din of the world's carried flesh———tree-fabric is transitional season, trains the rubric upon a transit of seizure

Local alignment betwinned at the symmetry's dash-through, permanent elisions ———a plantation left alone with its re-cranked pores, breathing the fleeing intervals

Probing (tooling) it as texture-use, robbing it of local reach———nothing left of a passage but its pass-over———the parallels shoot any correspondence through themselves———only the buffeted local with previous harms it did might slow up on these new delves

A fresh ease of compression, the wake everywhere, in anti-densities of neutral rebound———every duration is a public transform———adjoining leaves are figures of failed retake———side-shoots of a secondary (greened-up) positivity, how to grow unavoidal trees on these abrasive slopes

Contusive contours the denounced side of an unthrown thing, blocked currents re-randomised, these offspring are the clamped lurch of the line itself———projectile cohesion a space for racing its livery onto the snatch

Any sprint retasks us———what can it ask of the near of here?——— any larch would flutter this through its pre-imposed profile

The half-silence of unghosted interludes, will the armature of passing flex its temporary voids?———prayer crouches at a demarcation-post of pre-arrival———the vibration not yet even due, already spun from the spares of spiritual indigence

Grouting ahead of itself, fore-slidings in accurate prediction, no further derivation———these trees took their orderly rustle so far as their rind, skins of weather and time———local hardenings perform corrugations against seamless jets of injury

Stakes of ties, plantation mechanics landed across new contusions, observe direct asymmetrical access———precision glissades impossible to filter through a count of trees

Their grid was the prevailing imposition, beset leathery until hoary for inter-position enough, neighbour of co-densities———acceleration otherwise in refractive vanishings

Flight forwards towards overfull mission or empty session, horizontal buoying infests conduits of bankless betweens, the plantation asset its own rigid stalling———naked stems parade hack on block at the quicks of this pulsion staging them

Trees warty as only standing by———allowing wrapped surfaces some true local harm

Injection of streamline shaved mass at each super-cutaneous instant———for this incident, trees are the disconnected implement, ancillary recitals of green fluster, weedy disassociation

Heterogeneous loss-areas intermocking———serial trees confined by
their own carapace, much used protection not affording resistance

Where does acceleration harbour its thrown statics?———deposits
of relief as recondite griefs of the local———strewnness is ribbon of
counter-seclusion, previous overridings now face into a wrong bay—
——their backs exposed to a newer by raw

Expressive speed perfected where it can't leave a landscape kept under
woods———can't size it either, only mark it with its repeat-quittances

Plantation edges unruffled in their rinds, untrifled but totally rushed
upon———by a webbing with no local knots———total transmission
leaves nothing by way of residue remission

Incisive leap through a landscape it appends as shots at surface———
square that with the rinds, organic fronts of deformation, assemblies
of previous trials———rails are uncompassed information at this race
to scale———something in the earlier abruption (trees grown to rule)
misses the second, by a matter of secondaries

Plantation wreckage no primals either but exact horizons from the
shucked face of it———so perennial with constant travel quavering
(quartering) it———what is the final portion (exhaustion) of this new
systemic rumbling if not a harsh gradient (expedient) of tree surfaces?

Interpret the manifest behind a charged glut of trees, ruts of pure
transigence at central skimming———the rear shudder of a clean-
scoured willing band

A screen of short but endless purges, above enough speed devoured by
holding rail———upswing of a previous guardian whose branch is
empty sentry

On wings for the rake of it brushed, harsh fling full-on at unmistakable
wake———needle-rapid by means of forest vent———rapier-thin
sections of nil congress

Terse set-aside, only in line of it mount the spurs———any other root space frozen to the bypass-ditch in place of reprisal———rumours of bruised boundary endorsed with a speed sealant

Train-fleck by own memorial, plump corridor berates leaning trees, stranded intervals

Perfect perspective at speed as crossing crevices of capped deckage, micro-industrial greens

Former cuticles, erective shield in swathes rephased at stretch———apt surface, paced steerage, surly belated after-efforts of rind

The smaller the reset, the darker the sparkle———borrowed invariably, recliffed, lean wrangling for an unswerving route———every thread of the way pulled from its verdure registry

Imperfectly notched, unable to distance itself from its horny reach———an oak too near the lines of it, too sheer of contused spine

Reluctant interior marginals, the co-unvisitable onsets of spate——— raw with scattered hoops (tree rings), clumps are underlain latches, the offside thatches

Retasked wildings, cradled in second-rate presence———tapped of any disparate entwining accumulation———electric exhaust spends itself over the sprung allocations———how far can its interceptive intake harry the outrake?

Blockwoods as This: Not Unknotting

Nothing strangely
weaker that the
need for wholeness
—Stephen Rodefer

...but a virginity of being, ontological...in brief, to retrieve the primordial or original power of naming... to recover the brutality of beginning
—Olivier-Thomas Venard

As if to unlock blockade
or release it to its interferences,
on the way of, across the path of
at a staple arable of trees
the stamped root of assistance
is occupational

resistance at its sprung palliatives   vertical risk goes cagey over its fir extensives

amend a tree to its structural tabs, cramp it a co-attended   tokens of latitude, remitting chastened amplitudes

is the prevention: anticipates in block formation its ontological spurt (weight)   the sweep tarries until its own graining will have reached an across   to flow with each encapsulated stub

a reversion concession recodes (coats) the circling horizontals, is hood and cloak to a contrary compression, not one fleck looser

an ob/struct vents the green cascade   immediate rim rehearses a seating it immersed, thickly occurs across stripped

a leaner channel taps
its own vestiges, festoons
the pressure lock, stoppages
unblanked

how a runnel cribs its shoring   its through-to implants abreast,
punches (graces) butts of crustfilm, trimflow, groundflood

as the slippage is clipped with this, fetched at the sudden shutdown,
onset of sharp symbolic wastage, its spread (vantage) terrain
without which the secreted horizontals starve

constriction at the plunge itself bulges unknown envelope   unflowns
rake up and seal it plenty by vertical relation   diagonal breadth of the
post-open, preliminary meta-release

ample tumble trails the knot, on the exact spot   a basketed spire
whose pull encumbers each living wire   offskirted for a knot's inner
fringe

moored bulge not hulk grants body   its ropes at a covering of
unpaused germ   a range ahead of a lunge   disdains the fresh flesh,
re-cairns the crash of it,   the crush of its bulk becoming, becalming

banked / swarmed / harmed at the resting ferment   now a little
intimate with post-torment thew   the interlocking rudder is vertical
shudder   each surface shrinks (shivers) the contingents of another

climax plane at its embrace
again, vertical at depthless
relief bordering: fords
horizon knot over knot

acclimatised reserve, the binding only bold for lightest tendril   edge
rivets (enspirited) don't themselves alight   re: the co-blight of

what not yet let go set from margin towards sore ventral offer   on
behalf of a not yet shared non-release   knots will spot the entrance,
not increase   tether (allow span for) some membrane of reception

a tree's congestion hurtles
its shrubbing, requites unstealthy
verticals   truly nondescript once
unbroken in common choir

tender ruin qualifies for prediction, slenderness reassessed the rim,
no neuter is as chancing as steeps of this   spared horizontal at knotted
creep   scarce not rampant, collates the stickiness of behalves at
betweens

veins taller for lashes, spears of attachment, knots of fruition   befell
the provenience of implicity, total transfer *at* its clotting

loose, unslashed traps in
relay-trips   real otherness
which included them
around our own blockages,
green baggage

not trivial preventive, blocking
is deformable but embedded:
an unknot stuck at/is
its particular traverse
across the grain

a tangle diagram so blocked out as to label its leaf for airy minimal
touch   attachment by holding the miracle to its least

freedom continuous arc
tasking-over the crossing,
garment-fold group of a knot
its overheads relieve (relive)
block for block

the error of meaning it tree-prominent   duration of block averaging
already salvaging repletion at its blunter less possible, actual to a least

float block from blockade along a pacing-large arena   the quota is
natural wood distilled by each truss of the grain

the replication block only
solid at a leaf's horizon,
lone freefall to a treeful
of the unknot
that it wells to a through-blockage,
so untooled as shoulders to stand,
seeds no other casing

the terror of appealing the blockage tree-flung   spun onto its tauter
(uncropped) span to crown   put the batch-block to its own fresher
hitching, feed the seizure on its pivot

hoary tree-suds veer from surd, spurt horizon from their receptive
sealables   given in taller seams once the vast is crested and pendant

an average abiding stirring, thick blocks of the murmur   as filigree
does stretch impounding its density   prescience at a found (forked)
compound

a floss banded, convolute at one bound never again stranded   no
need of any future camouflage   diminishing as it shrubs, condenses
purposing to wood   drag of speck to braiding it, co-blading the spot

compaction legend of the trees' blatant swerve   substrate nostalgia
still recalling perimeters   by symbolic underload, rinse it replete with
lignin ligament

damaged propensity heals the liable,
only with this preliminary
blockade will anything adhesible
sow the pliable

staunchness of tree-mass not unique to the awkward hamperings of
block attracting (releasing) block   to lock in fresh oak a roaming
hue   gradient leap enchased in leaf   earth's burden lightened to a
tree cordon

tree-broad, blocks out
its spatial risk in onsets
dance horizon, insets
plugged to where they
curve with orbital task

blockwooden, an engirthed stiffness grows it upright   grist of micro-
rigids at the trees' peculiar flocking

a quanta of obstruction performs the interim's transition   beholds the
allegory of nurture to be fully leafed thus interferingly

at the tree horns they
block-mark to cap it,
each cellular inter-phase (upturn)
an outcome of hood

richly obstructed, trees have landed, not dumped the impact
touched by most alive thwarting, their degrees of prayer   stiff-decked
flight of trees, coagular sped

what decentres across is openly allocentred on axis   at a blunt
tangent fully shared, commonly impaired, the reparation instances each
reluctant gate

any impediment above ground is broader for root decorum   free
depth around the micorrhyzal dive

a blockage unwired at thickest vein, multi-spired   resorts to the
conduction it holds to, sparks the retentions

transcorporeal persistence   fidelity to the immediate modes of
obstruction (alignment)   keeps, overarches, doesn't reap

diffractive / infractive at the initial dark arc of a tree's patient swing
taken with its cramped shade before diffusing in aid   sluggishly
suffusion clinches the event of neighbourhood

whenever reception is
symbolic freight before it
can become exception,
acceptation: key mode of its
over-recouped intervals

how woodland blockade glorifies before it rectifies   will conflate one
occlusive remission upon the given recess of another

to rig out its own (unsown) debris   new woods on racks of the
blinding foretold,   each dedication within reach

clog the floods, encourage
what the woods will risk,
condensation in full-range
trafficking

the gel of unconcealed setting,
attentive indurities furnish
the phasings of a slope:
will test freshly remoting
(demoted) woodland shafts

pause saws at the protesting
creep, wood floor is the
initial enclave, archive

blocks as they wooden   a braid parading the stood   trees groomed
to their own non-removal, terse stilted backfade   already further
pounded than blasts of serial renewal

blocked from a neutrality of conversions   unavailable at the material
grant of repetitions unless the exchange radiates   a sharp socket
prints, its includings branch (reclude) this bracket

as tree curtains will hang out the roots, not drying but to hoard the
fetchments

how a tree-block rolls from pinched drag   accommodates a rotation
of soil, needle grooves sound steeple

blocks of indentation unnumbered, a tree-crowd is vented everywhere:
the inter-cession of pitched resistance

detect a parallel order or
not be grievous   any shut closet
is worth its tree-saddle

a raw sum in pine option, newly out of stay, block-ridged
tailored limbs of unscaled fellow summits   micro-blocks are the
overlap of apex shingling

the ratchet of these under-tagging woods   shouldering its symbolic
pardon   from blockade to attuned berth   it alleviates the knot
constellation   their block profile

such collective custody is not accessionary here   trees fling bright
blockade, exfiltration has no further barrier   pastoral won't field its
reserve without this callousness of trees

emboss cared spaces
through block within block:
quanta insistent until
reprieved at jolt

blockwood as in skin-swarthy,
grazed proficient   density
surfaces are spoken from

a racket of tree-clinch at the hop and scoop   the counter-weakness of
a proto-lesser   verticals initial the histories of it

when trees become blocks of themselves for remedy   no such chaste
greens on impact   what their givenness does clumps them at full
ontological barrage

obstruction, retrenchment   actual carrying of one frame across
another   make their most sinuous shots at horizon

within fleetness of the stood,
hints and burdens, nearer
clearance would not be
for their guise

the forest once unleashed still won't have overtaken its original hutches:
rucked crease prowls any callow advance

what tautness
at once brought short
combs its fidelity
to horizon?

reliant by wild re-warding   accumulates behind any other forefront,
staying bower is the last non-isolate

trees to their racks are not the ongoings of the species   bough
intransigence itself presides, assists, attends   no such relays in
evolution but local co-volitional   it isn't genus which is the regreening

block elements come with various fill and shading   end-of-proof a
tokening for tree-roof   if symbol exude interceding blockage, let it be
at an icon vector   tacking, caching, perpetual stillage

is a plantation's configurable any sort of ritual formative, elected cohort?
commons of liturgical density, compromised immensity?

open summits heed (arc) the frankness of tree   non-clearance the
forwarder towards an horizon instep

block attribute in guttered symbols (seams) of co-affinity   exact
stopping-off point (attuning station) at this gamut

multiple blocks (not this
received cluster) nest
in the source mode,
nearest scope

local symbol at its rugous (rayed) block-specifics   the wood cove is
hollow enough, shielded valid

impossible to put weight on an earth were it already tree   no block
alive could so derive its rate of loft

block resonance (crescence) the relay motif, relief long before vestiges
let an armistice of shelter retemper heavy cladding

a movement without rupture from one growing position to another,
the sequences contrive pivot, pilot

naturalisation no neutrality in mast architecture   prayer stirs at
chiming alongside scale (scowl) of block   inordinate readiness for
contemplative receipt

at each block deeply
inscribed marks of season:
horizons of the trees'
(en masse) proposal

what frank symbol condenses   blockades find/lend its lightning
deposits,   forest glint giant-banded at core   splints of induration

to engage (kindle) joint is to manoeuvre local rigidities   find the exact
latitude of branch

revealability that won't coil (enwrap) its way through blockage unless
it can be sealed (scaled) at intact burden of the given   as chunked
(wedged), does reveal the such, how it weathers, furthers, translates

truth self-pounded, unconditional or grown at its own confess-the-
height   at every compress of averring horizon let tree

Note

This poem attempts a near impossible task: to speculate on and fabulate pressures/pressings of symbolic receptive activity: burdensome or clotted or transformative bearings/nearings implicit in all life and offerable at this extending/burdening of its/our words.

Surfaces the Deeper the Oak

A tree is not
one. When a tree
is severed
a world departs
Anne Elvey

That they may be called oaks of righteousness…they shall raise up the former devastations
Isaiah.61, 3-4.

I

Severed oak portions   butt heads or rump
joints steeped in (stripped to) their distributing new surfaces   only such
sheared faces could combine this razing-through of ruin by ruin

brackets of root-oak, two basements off stack strapped
to own cuts   mutilated edges ground to a relief shower,
what comes to be thrown (known) over a surface

five faces of severance and a detached root-cradle,
new bare faces against the shallows, the latest
deep rending sweeping more than their own lie-out

squat joints kneeling on a platform of destitution,
cradling a fresh banter of root-reliant ratchet,
deadly snatches will be a surface's prime mutation

surfaces scraped against their own skin,
any fold of it grazes radical intrusions

new edging on a scoured shelf, surfaces dashed against surface
(whether upright or prone)   a heavy openness
without departures

here the oak-scraps (steps to what they gave) proclaim
their residue   a scabby, uncupboarded reminder,
tree agenda desiccated, dedicated

sand and spoil foam on a black parapet of tree,
against welterless grain comb the
before and after of an oak

the oak doesn't wish itself shed but remains ahead
of the levelled graze   how many sprung levels from
five faces (multiple seasons?) off severed joints?

an oak in its abandonment stickless and spikeless

where at once hands and feet of a tree's alighting
ransack the contours   oak unclenched assures new surface strides,
tree riddance offers further knuckled trajectories

oak surfaces don't move but do exert tilt   all what a
right/left rocks across dirt-floor imposition   which will have been
shoved beyond its native engineered tremor

off many severed planes these unpropped fragments
offer a naïve regard, bad frontage   become a dawning of
surface beyond surface from a depth of helpless exposure

II

Braiding its destruction to fund any crevice   anything a
cashed-out surface can't string out but with more than
dust expedition to retrieve

here nothing surface-suspended remains fluid   a dusting (flush with
itself)
is offered the pain of newly unplaced crags,
parts of an oak spying out

no such teemings among discarded uprights   severed joints
won't be further abbreviated, awkward
bandings imperil the plains

elementary credentials not posing this clearance as landscape,
oak chokings its non-sedimentary counter-host:
a tree's vertical layers can be so exposed, parodied

such rips demand an unknown quota of absorption,
quartered tree-plates won't otherwise be revoked

cuts, new stances of rejection, become the surface targets of
re-section   fresh brackets of forest detection, static insurrection

although rigidity was the estimate (oak lined) it was
as a steeper twisting of land whose surfaces
did more than wheel to unwind

these bones were the cabled stoop from summit   once
so smattered on a level there will be no more
unattended signal surfaces

green stallings (stalkings) in quest of surface rind   what
amends ruin is residual grinding, the nested
gestures of shock

once this featured (futured) derision of oak splays out
instructions (off its own division rind) there will be
no further pause

imploring what has already craved tree-stain   oak pegs
parallels on a vernacular surface   no other gain

a marker-face at interior departings   particular
separations are paid for at the rate of
surface bleaching, retrenching

new contingency of post-arrivals (smote the oak)   now a
tauter necessity of pre-surface, columnar soil,
remote embedding

available parts at the thin of it   tree chunks will never be
slender again but render squandered soil readily
a pleading between goaded surfaces

brute organics not lodged but smudged upon soil   already an
outline of unforeseen reversions

remnants forsaken at a fuller domain's skewed spread   the fallout
(surface) compromises any riot (rest) of singulars,
risks its own horizontal indemnities

oak fragments strangely swathed in stratum garb, convert the
order of abandonment   these savage exeats
are accurate deflectors

creasing a surface with tiers of ribbing   no oak-fall
will alter the accentuations

surfaces sweated out at speed grope their way towards
broken oak   naked station for vertical pulses   a trounced gutter
lying *over* the arena's spend-offs

the surface can't but drag across itself this outer
rocking, intensive capsize

an oak-hulk to be smashed (sensed) but not pecked
through   these remains are the sole bite
a scoured surface has irritability for

pooling (not stirring) undragged studs across an
over-sealed (rolled) surface in kind

the centre (counter) of a bestrewn body, this is what
pure surface awaits, as if tree wreckage
becomes a vent

oak separates gave off no shimmer   it is bare soil
must swim them, be flooded at them   hooding and gusting
is a surface tide bound to oak

what a tree won't recant is what it makes shunt along
the flats, rumble of a contrary muster

where surface wastes are the new wavering   ground entrustment
of a few transcript fibres   however spread across, no surface
can level (substitute) a sidestem

unremovable rejects, no further conscripts, here clearance
is left to its own witnesses

as the oak had left no shutters the new tooled surfaces must
simulate them   remaining stubs will ventilate
beyond any horizontals within reach

to trust deep tree clemency, its root the first outshot
of the breach   this beaching is not
its least resource

scarcely extant oak, nothing but
upright camouflage

what scouting of grounds ahead for chopped (untrapped)
oak?   every other surface accordingly raw, chapped
with the dead verve of unusable transition

haunches of oak uninsulated, what they dent of the floor
confides its own poachmarks, the hitches
at every new gravelling

from the first plain of arrears (clearance) so many tree surfaces
yet to come   how they cast their booms across
currents (trials) of dust

as if two nodes of broken oak could offer leached surfaces a
new coating   from where the clearance novelty pleads to
coagulate, compromise meets unrecognised root effort   a depth
proficiency
even at its crusty surface arcing

scoured tableland with no other vibration than disporting oak

immobilised flocks of blanched detritus but no docking   untrussed
tree-parts not drifting

a shallow subsoil has become superspoil off tree
deckage   admits vertical multiples, unconditionals of an
erasable aptitude marking its sole rejoinder

bail-out for a broken tree is to swim onto its new
surfaces, keep them afloat

compressed verticals distress (address) compliant
levels of passage-work

systemic (anti-invasive) patterns are this signing pittance of oak,
inwardly hiccups where it can't intercept

how many radical surfaces previewed on the stump-mirrors of
severed joint?   how a worksite quivers, at deposited tree-trash
is appointed its own buckling

as broken (absent) crown it can't overtake the crests of
surface   its phantom height will crunch the levels,
recurl them

III

Oak offcuts gather the surface but can't grade it,
they are its starkest concession   rubbish made rare to available ground,
new soils begin over this costing

focal brink a token of their unlack   taken into their nonstock   new
sacrifice surfaces remind old veinings of
their burden of nurture

thinnest participation of vertical terrain (root/crown)   had always
pierced (spared) the surfaces   given them evidence
of their riper furnishings across

clapped on unswathed soil but not cased by it   stranded tree backfire
trawling surfaces until they rewrite their barest
calm in arboreal prefaces

a broken tree saves without rallying threadbare surface   nil
oscillation but the brittle poles of height and depth
at every further plan of debris

this litter damage was always oak   newly traded to its own set
deforms   surface transfer won't sprinkle it
without reseeding its own clearances

how a trash of deep spine lies in wait   smashed oak rests on its
radical incline, no stronger tilts   abets a future crust desist from
the site's speed of sieve, corridor layout

at hunted oak its dry seeps of congruence, exemplary
protuberance   eventual upright hinterland

oak-tomb a slab on a surface it amends   rootless and crownless
summons refigured expanse   such losses of overhang
surfaces will have expacted (drawn down) enough to
reset standing concessions, re-site contusion

the bleak torso angled to future contours   any remainder a
converse capture   these swiped levels have yet
to gyrate for forest bearings

due monotony of the clearance will break formation   an oak's
primordial lift is not sealed along sideways sifts   among such wreckage
it is surfaces will unzip themselves

sheer transit spread of clearance has resurfed at its known obstacle
course   gets thrown over integral hurdles

sawn stem retrieves variance along its own intersection   the
interruption
does what a levelling might learn from ever finer mesh   vertical
exception ordain broadest reception

oak outlyers, self-etched, pared down according to most acute
transformation   how surface prays its unders and overs   vertical
singularities will guide the retro-faction
of stranded tree

ironic a smashed oak doesn't go against grain, moulds it,
regranulates it, how a non-absorbent ruin must bulge the seams
spinning its former prow, the accordance
of a hem of prayer

for chafing nearer this abject sacred site, despite no
grateful limb   a site slipping its steps
where waste oak had rucked it

codeless but stricken enough to interpret these flaunted
levels   they do the lineation but not the
depth debts of width

oak: from non-necessity to super-impression: surfaces
called up at their own other
(even taller) dimensions

tree-ruins sheltering what they ran out with   final
fragility of what will breach (peak) the closure
of sufficient surface

what is the itinerary of kernel (spurned) oak if not to reknit every
side (size) of available surface?   one brittleness will embolden another,
smashed oak, branded land

dereliction will be gaunt projection beyond its remainder
layouts, towards new cross-sections of surface

oak wasn't initial but original-secondary   surface
recursionaries which pure horizontals
don't recoup alone

disabled tree is another form (persistence) of intention   stricken
motives which surfaces must
quicken and spiral

such oak pieces are not scaffolds but shock-screens
blown forward, imaging squalls
of future fold

surface can't survive as the crowd of itself   steepens against
a borrowed rebound off two ruins,
the site's retrieved membrane

a confusion (confession) of levels fetches forest   twin recessions
of oak will have an horizon's penitence (penury):
with tree-hips laid on soil, surfaces can
no longer cheat decayed verticals

at the horizons of their exploitation, see these immediate secondaries,
a ritual of broken oak

what has been strewn and not repackaged is ultimate
reserve   bones (how browless) are a counter-dimensionality:
realigning every other surface on which they
no longer stand upright by themselves

oak aptitude at its most radical disconnect   with cropped roots on
ungainly show this flailed HS2 sector will have scored
a terminal rebranch

Note

Passing the newly enlarged HS2 Compound near Stoneleigh in Warwickshire I was struck by two basal fragments of felled oak on the verge of a freshly stripped bare-earth terrain and went back to have a further look. I became haunted by how the fragments seemed both rejected and alert even to being on the watch, a sort of bifocal tree-remnant no longer complying with any particular prevailing surface. Arcing brokenly forward towards/between the multiple surfaces (depths) of wronged relations, strayed corrections, stationary revisions.

Trees as Lived

(Some Retorting Legends)

With grateful acknowledgement to Robin Walter, 'Living With Trees', (Little Toller Books, 2020)

A massive vanishing that remnants not finding their displacement
haunt the native sacrilege   until flushes of niche
frequent the canopy

Well-confined islands, common colonisers   small stands against
no other woodworld   how bark wedges itself
onto humanscape

Essential projection if trees are to become ancient   few
insistences slower than old trees

Accrued niching at bodged clearances   an irreplaceable is
sapping human speeds

Invasive afforestation, lodge it with pines, engross the
uplands   nothing sparse about the correctness offered
its pole pressure

Any tree-total upland is tireless, swathed in indurate
spoil, horizontal furling, sitka comprehensives

Geometric blots, felled or poisoned for exotic replant   locust
years (yields) leaching the ancient woods   starkest
shapes pay on distant funds

Too young for wildwood or semi-ancient remnant, squarely
a distinctive teeming?   are there any late promises
for these plants?

Saplings holed-in graduate no forests   busily enmeshed
in an unremoved unthrived network

Tree damage itself key stowage for curdling the web,
such reinforced threads strung into repointing their
breach marks   drag an incantation across
its ecological ceiling

As emergent trees chip out our repression creases   create a city
of their markings as remission of seize

As hedgerow commutes, clump replete, seeking a
rate of tree *outside* the woods   surviving as timber,
reviving in pollard   serves (calls at) what is
no longer husbanded

stitched by us, patched by nature   tab-edges between the
farmed slabs   however a woodful additive, befits shelter

cracks and edgelands a justified elsewhere, filtering in the
midst of dilating like for like

Homicidal air locks onto trees, at net weight of carbon   strict
riddance of forest by blossoming streetly aside

Block planting at its default position   equity is most of
the least, ensuing scarce verticals   farming tree as public good/s
urban forest retrofit

As the generic cellulose factory speaks cheap land   locality
deficit, less a neighbourhood than its own notionals

Then to scatter a copse at its join-ups, the more social its
scarcities, the more frond-like its secretions

The empty song-shock of *not* encountering a tree,
forest echoes follow the flatter rumble of
baffled townscape

Life isn't muted enough to faint before all its details,
leaf-lendings, edge-plummets

A quotient of symbols as altered image, the danger-range of
emphatic statics

Hint of oak roof marking with suburban spraint, there was
always sufficient hutting until the wooden became its own
excess structures

No rougher supertide than a surface's reverie of buried
conservation, striating its dust   live chainsaw culture
climbing trees, an impactive speckling of species

Walk a grove through a welter of woodland   where arrivals
are monitored and wrapped   newly aproned into extension

Play wild lime where it stood   a scarred towards, a lesser as
at last forewarned

Stunted, instantiated, post-solo stress redolent of trees at rest

Expressive forest at the toe of ancient tree   a tumble of assent,
assignation, reception, within a single throw

Pervaded (circuited) before any surface annunciation,
the eruption event then has no need to break out
for cover

What is the character that enters a wood as the wood's own unsown
persona?   then ranged, assailed, at every available tree-height

Take a cut from forests flourishing?   the languishing clearfell
furniture until the woods fulfil different weeds

Buffeting and sinking woods where graspable   to relieve
their core interior, rebestow their corridor files

What else might haunt trees other than our epic scale?   as forest
sores to carbon stores

Grown as if (to be) last, it escapades its own exhaustion

What stunts at the figures of juicy trees, a sap of all surges at
the stripped bark

Tender green argues specific pasts, tests (grains) the subtler
proofs   if any web of causation stands to every
least consequence

A barrage of stress, that it rubs out puckers of instress,
knotty intrication not yet couplings, underseam
ripples

Leave at its loneness how hollow trunk synchronises with
stag head   woods continue their cycle on the most
difficult ground

There is an increment how trees are put by for a decade, a
quota of anterior consideration, narrative of a
rerooting at loss

Not every wood needs a great habitat industry   dense and
dark may shed some diversity but go pastoral at the
edges of asperity

The worn scrub its own exhaust against super-use turbulent garb

Proforest, entire sports of tree initiative   instinctive gaps, continuous
interlude: or *implanted* tree would already be
on its damage slant

At a stitch of tree entwine the shoots of local faction, itself
a decompaction

Landscape services redesired, as recompiled under unequivalent
trees

Expand if it thins   more diverse onto its adjacencies,
distinctive assemblages, these effigies invoke a healing
parody, prayer-rooms of nested induction   for the urging climate,
aspen, oak, hornbeam, lime

Wintry Forests, Old Trees

Brushwork, a parting met with, casual unconstricted inflection,
a branch that spares so little of a time but shares its alignment

to twist (trust) the soaring is to meditate the veer
a learning grip on a guiding place
loaned array of instruct the way

wintry forests their gullied reaches traced
like a stricter mist, glint of a perfectly firmed peril
at its seasonal awning winter trees at an aura of warning
expresses hard the shadowed reasons of life

the winter grove a near contemporary of naked hiding
as harsh forest pulls deep into its cloak,
how the winter copes a skin akin to itself

dead hollow trunk no less fond
of the smallest twig the fan from one to the other won't be shallow

wrecked or broken beyond their expedience,
faring a further obedience not driven
beyond season in terms of it,
a curse which prays its scar

creates inexhaustible bushiness, trance of
indented body whose are the intimate counterparts
to winter stiffness, trees at length after the blow

never alike but often approximate,
leaves contrive their stalks to thrive few
witherings which their own leaning
doesn't seclude, seeing the human into itself,
leafing blunt neighbours

this wintry structure of brushline is its
thermal abbreviation, weak currents enwrap pines
at the level distance of their isolation,
the cage of winter solidifies the insulation

spindly terraces, kindly/spiky ease
of the tenuous   sweepings of prayer
as prayer is to its kindling disappointments,
prayed into what they outcome most widely

whose durances steer their worn hangings,
the slenders refresh elements of nature,
in leafless trees beguile dry branches

shattered green by a thousand fears
from its rotted (rooted) hulk   a finely stemmed
art at its deepest pine   patches
of wound are props against sagging

brevity of human life, a levity of network
saving the shadows along branches   old trees
bent, recurrent, still put up ramps for scattered leaves

the gnarled imagery borrows trees to survey it,
a smaller tree retouches its depth by
crossing in front of main pine

a style of tree-figure trembles at what
its brushwork might have seen   without
slighting a season's screen sealed in repairs of green

wintry themes testify a bunching tree-fan's
unknown follower, crystalised allowance:
impart to the trees their mood of standing,
codes of pine set in rock itself in song

how this brushwork rolls, thinning but
winning its shimmering effort difficult embrace
will distinguish tree contour from entire rock

old plum or pine jagged as rock, its stark
silhouette strums with graphic harm,
twin pines level for distances, is their
calligraphic precision, lyric elision

rocks and trees do intend crevices
but one great pine attends to sealing
the clan, relations with small plants

to be old is probable larch, strewn guardians
of signature rock, enigma attaches wintry integrity
of faint green on pine if groves (piled snow) seem
to flock here, what circumstances
are they returning?

twinned pines were done as gift, sent
far away, without bending pride in
massing or flickering, looming
indebtedness before winter chill

cloudy forest, brief pressure of branch-ends
together, unmistakably leafless, twisting
all four directions, how hoary bark interacts
while feathering at pulse these alarms
make room for lesser plants

to speak of the youth of wintry forest,
to mention an early season, not ages of wood

prayer of participation a winter's partition,
solely a loaned prayer at the visited beacon

cindery forests despite (due) cold trees,
tree-tall for exhibited station, winter collation:
tree-poor and a wind biting winter's ledge

rushed by snow, pressed by frost, these habits
bend down their majestics   the legacy
on mulberry bark   random indications
prone to nature, obvious abstractions,
precise parallels

too few leafless trees but seen among
flourishing forests   that they be held to turn away,
no abundance in branch, tips set back, not let go:
how habits of tree remain open on as many sides

open or sprawling, a slightness of tree
taken aback   elderly tree, perhaps already dead
but supporting lives in the still,
explaining vines and flowers

oldest oak on short staff   as the sun goes down
marsh reeds desert a view from the mountains:
late autumn sky, silver tracery of leafless trees,
orthodox departures idyllic as windblown

branches' bare silhouette, without descriptive
subtlety   commoner centre, gnarled weathered
ink-strokes exist the simpler
at its own shadow or peak?

delicacy on a hill, branching as their twigs, an intimacy
of nature under eaves   late scenic spots
beside a shattered tree   the void of its apartness,
a music of heaven   leafing out
to what it had lost by the lengths of it

sensing in the old tree something
(propagated) of the oldest known

prayer shoddily autotelic   participates
roughly enough to seek being intended
among old trees: address amended by what
the spirit offers not to return from, neighbour rock

prevailing mutability taught to
winter itself   respite within
rigour, the new mutuality?

tremulous figments of
allegory innovate within
their wintry cage

no mirage of external
clearance, winter erasure,
but starker congregation

hard appearances imprint
their screen, none
are empty shells

less dull or shut up
than any neat spruce:
now sprung to its
winter observance

as winter stands proxy
for unwounded leafage
to come, bare composure
forwards the event

enduring rock/staunch pine:
what is standing with/for:
crisp/sharp or gentled
stalk, each is allegory of
the other's found winter

the feeling (bearing) of going
briefly onward   quiet trimmings,
natural presence is itself,
taller habit witnesses hemmed
the allegory from itself

neighbourhood forms of its
prayering's scree of place

how the world is, less precarious
unshaded   in shaggy stipple
offers its inferences, sus-
pended sustenance

retraction is at last the spirit's, a tendril's implicit density

Sources

This poetry derives from and draws on 'Wintry Forests, Old Trees: Some Landscape Themes in Chinese Painting' by Richard Barnhart (New York: China House Gallery, 1972, (kindly lent to me by J. H. Prynne) and J. H. Prynne, 'The "Night Vigil" of Shen Zhou', *SNOW lit rev*, 2 (Fall 2013 – Spring 2014), 94-114.

In Givens Greet the Donation

The gifts made to us are the anticipation of a gift that they promise to us. The character of promise is the perpetual stimulus of donation beyond the finitude and vulnerability of the given. (PD 160)
—Jean-Yves Lacoste

1
To unreserve its task again
never less free of its husk,
the basking antecedent

2
Material disclaimer
is the foretime of
an already's donation

3
Cast the abyss, its lips
were the uncertainty,
a world's skim was
scouring through us

4
Initial glue of the less than
real not yet spurned across
inclusion, emerge to
a pre-ajar seclusion

5
Emergence least decoded
by antecedents, horizon
a remnant, entry of the becoming,
a late having been given
primes being-for at gift

6
A gracious storm on the
tongue, unmuting tasks of the
synthetic, common mesh
of the after-span is turn
within spools of the before

7
Awoke to greet cumbersome
stars, that they might
gravitate the radiance
of so few remembered slumbers

8
How slender limbs poke
into a where, a care of tree
stalking, condensing off a
crouch of sky

9
To select loss against its
mark, the trunk sprung
from its stealth of indirections,
given to testaments of the
lack, abrupt re-donation

10
Roaming the sticking paces
of coagula, how fabula loans
the whole range, sprint histories
across a swivel of norms,
the axle of donation

11
A bruise unbracketed on leaf
despite ringing out veins in the
salience, sentience is reserve
absorbance, shielded witness

12
The body inseparate from its turn
of an innermost before core,
the outer host of horizon

13
Rear the forms between roots
staying in stride of eventually,
a constant of a future full
rotation upon a pre-given

14
Moving in on some engagement
around coding a tree,
its depth charge in layers
of partaken leafing

15
In seams more confederate
affront the near, how the
universal non-return prays,
loads an already granted
to a pitch of donation

16
This caress for shudders at a time,
follow surfaces holding one
horizon within another's re-
cession at the reception itself

17
So strikes an act of givens
in unique donation, how prone
is any future to the stretch
(latch) of unique origin this

18
Echo a face thrown forward
at unexpendable push, givens
of no fate but what is drawing
on its unconditionals

19
A bluntness of the body but
swivelling outset, free verticals
of no further flicker

20
Wild grasses thrown from the world
as they reweave their threading,
beads in gift of horizon to seed

21
Like shells resorting to chambering
at the turn of an issue, in gift
of some new converse flow, meta-
dependence, ascendance

22
A rota bladewidth lattice of grace
does throng, swerves across (shaves)
its dawn thickness on the turn,
summons such expected
forsakens apprised, enacted

23
If not liturgy in the trees
none other in meticulous breezes
where metaphor swirls
on its ground

24
Off a scheme of trees
pendant futures of the traverse
not yet as green as
the already given

25
In guise of a row of trees,
a single pivot of meeting
another grant from the same
standing, in givens
of the new acuteness

26
Imparted in faint blisters,
awoken to late clusters,
horizon arises at the reflux
or what is tidally regauging
its unhold within enfolding

27
Kinship thrown up by its dust
co-ranging a day of thirding,
what hasn't turned so we
might, only then horizon
no longer twists, fully
wheels (prays) additional links

28
A tide of initially issued
giving scant need to the world,
self-dispelling borders harsher
than any bevel from origin

29
Fetch the havens of the given
to live the brunts (em/braces)
off the keen edges of donation

30
Emerge trammelled, harboured,
at every non-negotiable connector,
a transperson's take on the ante-
cedent, its gulf/grant a vast-
ness at the scarce difference,
exact gyre of the inherence

Note

Can anyone/anything address this ontological paradox? How what emerges across a deep time/space intermesh is greeted by a uniquely swivelling nexus of the already given unable to arrive until sensed before some pivotal horizon of recognition, in its single swerve, after which everything transitory is on behalf of, shares in a call to actuality.

A Stubble Like Stars

(after Jaccottet)

Comme si les derniers signes devaient venir du plus insignificant
—Philippe Jaccottet

Empty fields with no haste, an
ample almost colourless sign of life

Prevail a distrust over the too weary,
as a weightless avails the fragile

If the light was an absent designation,
no question of faking that shadow,
the lessened in its darkness

In zest of a kind of prelude,
tinkling of a message defied,
an appeal fully applied

No grace of herds or troughs,
given this altitude of effort

More than merely agreeing with
this cold anchor, so few noises
possible to my heart

Chestnut woods sheltering, small
(tall) stone constrictions pose there
as long in time, nest
of a slope, wing of a transform

The bristle of crown arisen far above
threat, like the pleats of tense foliage

A detour of telling the walk,
old age engraves my doubts on capable
surprises, captures of want

Small herds or even a pen
of trees, rounded limbs, written veins

Without any exclusion still a
non-immersion, the prolonged sanction
(sanctum) of remorse at peace.

Preference of the attentive,
exempt comparison

A mark (ray) of the breach
filters out the frail absurd

A slide of things illuminating the cradle,
this non-imitation of it settling
under a misted sun

Incredibly sheltered as little fashioned,
how ferocious for anything valid,
any prime marvel?

Busy caverns within an unscathed enclave, not admiring its own shadows, a few clouds ever-changing and so non-voluntary, scarce travellings of the goodness on the outer side of the window   collapse by chance of escaping unharmed, how fallen twigs build up a surface, minute ramparts of a renewed expanse   a sufficient but handless version aggravates the risk, these evasive undoubtfuls a remote pre-spring   scattered dawn of an announcement in the midst of very brief swarms, almond and apricot the expected gust, a reverie of no further hostility

Out of tune hope, quivering the
final rest, disquieting footsteps, whence
flying by the snow of it

Thinnest threads the silver branches are
snowing, knowing the unbearable,
its many coats

The ever-ordinary chapel, belated
sacredness, scourings of prayer, modest
free residue: its pre-resumé of
the initial crypt

To be too really dead to face the non-
voice of the fright neither wave
nor stutter, or whatever
will help heaven

A quince orchard, in open
concentration of the infinite,
unthinkable crossing of 'and yet'

II

They would fall silent, not evade
the matter, the way they were spaced,
as if new to the species almond

Swarm, spume, snow, bare white mist suspended above an earth still grassless, scarcely getting lost, the trees disarm the thought, provoke communion in their glimpse of bare soil   a brief murmuring alighting there, no grudge against greenery   utterly ordinary, or to seek too far from our paths   a life different from ours because it unfolds a spiralling, from bare branches to blossom   the fleeting fruit stain before it can be effaced,   the orchard retracts any image, is behind us now, travels the only ground scarcely, what it floats is its own standstill

I stand on my guard further and
further afield but drawn back to
no other possession, dreaming
the less of it

Crossing a threshold unimpeded,
carried away onto the dearth of it,
not stemming a profusion
of caresses

An unweighable under the auspices
of so many scales, changes of level
behind the trees, the blemish of
being compelled to approach

A feeble vestige of non-
indifference, a familiar spirit
meandering the intuition

Like infinity trading some invisible
dimension of the ritual, sole
plumage, face of an orchard

A first greenery graining the ground from its dust above, faint shadows of trees, the stare of it binding and agile, like the sport of a curtain externalising the play of effacement   a fragile obstacle (plant) sown against a wall, all those closed ties in the soil   a certain obscurity conciliated, not prescribed   the resisting secret of the sacred stumbles the imaginary, reproaches its shadow, of which the blossom not so paltry

Luminous spurts, the unknown,
remote nurture awaiting the unborn

To plough possibility for its field,
provisional without spurning, a porous
fulfilment thrown from destruction

In a dust (soot) of words, beneath a
particular sky, remote and afflicted
(affiliated) in what is seen across
a marvel glimpsed

The eye of some analogy scans the sky,
liable to a slightest thing, how branches
confuse snow with lingering blossom

Renounce a rate of obvious meaning,
blossom become that cloud of snow
over an overcast sky, nothing
in waiting

some sort of outcome conceded to
the frontier of it, splinters alive
at an irritation of some
other dimension

III

The errant left so little, losing space
to present earth's distances

Death unseen amid winter's surviving
grass, hidden and patient threading
throughout a day (open field)
to be settled

Growing clarity but indistinct beneath
glass, a shimmer disdains hanging there,
on the cusp of a promise, dawn's
memory of a tear

Transferred alongside the green wood,
earth so easily scared of winter's ending,
a smoke (not a tomb) of the soul

Here where the earth draws its nearest merge
to a close (God between fantasy and stone):
the snow's fleeting light

Hanging in the branches a unique
belt, winter light on tree-bark,
love widening the dawn past its flash of axe:
without trespass a glimpse of God

Spiked above us now the heaving mountain   we can only watch and pray   freezing the stabbing, a blade buries stars in living flesh, birdsong merges with a dared scarce pity   rending and ripping more than knotted in air, dissolution is a heavier lash, at last the crash mountain-like in its airy thinness: a single grass seed, a mote travelling a knot in air, dusk and dawn leave no trace of the sound, a voice unspilled but slicing its single moment of pure day   already no longer a spindle but shuttling the darkening of the day, reserving links (chinks) of space which peer beyond my eyes

A quantity of being our knowing
nothing, which clings like paddock
and prairie, hovers the grave (grass)
over our silent invitation

IV

Born of dirt but no dull verging, flimsy
but hidden, violets break up the last snows of winter,
an upright liturgy a little more eternal
than this shift of shadow: don't speak loudly
of what sprouts from the earth

Detours efface mistakes, light fragile shots
from shadowy non-destructions at
the end of winter, violets
the capable tender tips

Nothing else yet something very different,
lowly things were needed to go further:
opening a way dark and cold, not too frail
to heed the replacement, a relay
of pathbreakers

Rechristen these flowers, my eyes
saw them removed into the network
of the world

An airy nave's array (tall oak) calms
any steps across its threshold   white spots
waver an unfloating mass of grass, unlikely
forms of life too nearly human   surge them
from the far reaches

Less bright constellations sort these
sparse umbels, less fixed once the day's
veil (beautiful) has withdrawn from
the trees' overhead response

Fragile galaxies (wild carrot) float across
a threshold of grass sky, a milk-white
within arm's reach, no sharp single stars
snagged on gorse

Whispering umbels, distinct or
linked to another hatching?   glimmer of
strange language hovering over the commons,
dawn chirping, shade and grave

A few umbels networking the shade of
tall greens, the restive forever-way
of the world's home

Bird unbound, a relic jewel close to
these relative half-heard words
left to the reeds and willows

Speak the pale blue and orange fragments of a world, a gaze's kingfisher slighted by its tender concern at the very last time   a lucky day in November, second life seeing the import of a fire vanish in the willows, once would suffice but do not aim for it: feathers flash singly among the reeds

Unite heart and wing in feathers
mocking the flash   what suffices is that it
led you out, as sun and sleep remember

V

Not blossoming but fruit laden
on the far side of wheat, the cherry tree's
no desire to win over, any encounter
another kind of story

Meaning little once abstracted
from its spot, so chanced upon a remaining
silent, as prayer questions its expectation,
of a heaven turning away

Fragments of joy convince the explosion
luminous like an inner star, and so to chance
upon sparkle, entire as revery, a
less than fruitless

A moment of grace not quite the upper
hand but muting any sense of separation,
inside things rise from the dirt path, like
a blade from the very field
it will scythe

Transition between day and night, fossil light
farthest of the links remaining   red cherries
within dark green, the semblance slumbers
(appears) at a silent metamorphosis.

A red not blood though standing cherries to the far side of their field, no broken branch but a fire breaching barriers of space, beckoning its restive remove beside a source of joy   emberless red, how dark green will flow as hung crimson, not biting what it blends   softens what will cluster globes moist for the night falling

Linked to the night's unheard river,
the far side of a field where no midst
ceased to be a path

A pillar (tame blackened fire) quivers
the leaves of its shelter, all suspense has slipped
into cherry, the small votive monument:
a decorated song I have lived, trembles the very
crimson I had pronounced laden

One colour within another (green to
red) is the moment of transition on its
own slow relay

Appeasing the arching of leaves, shelter
most like a sleeping festivity

No need to merely enter to quench that
breath of wind, footsteps wait
on another inclination

Did anything happen, not holding out
against its prayer?

VI

The little quince orchard sees (frees) another thing sheltered, that the secret of the world can't be grasped otherwise than tossed in the air, where what we can't enter is exactly what is at stake   solider swarms, opaque to be born or surge forth, the undeniable quiet of present flowering   if fugacity beneath those branches, then not unsettling the fragility simply there   barely white, the flowers seal a rose onto their tinge of waxy milk, less perishable than a woe anticipated, the tree a voiceless green room praying all by itself

White and green all along the colours, to be
closest to nature to be dull to be shy   mingle
freely the blows of flowers with the wound of leaves,
heals the enveloping

As if movement no longer enlisted
quiet shudders against
concealment

A generosity half-hidden in the grass,
the slow pace of a source of milk   transparency
forgets itself once it is more tender than
water, benignly thickening

Greenery is most mysterious appeasement,
what a temporary shelter advises, expresses

Slightest greeting, voiceless promise,
remembering how a correspondence in flight
is passing the skies

In imitation of leaves meeting their own
quiet-enough that conceals the sky

Summons a bare final echo, an extent
not to be caught at a limit unless
a fragile cage silent in the water,
a foliage cup

Higher heaven *is* as grass-coloured as this, community
of the burgeoning ghost

VII

Things as they really were, groundsel, hogweed, chicory like a child in times of old   or along a meadow no room to drop any mask, how its fate surprised me, in bloom   blue, yellow and white (the morning visibles)

mute the jubilation, caused by so little if not the incomprehensible,
mystery of the lesser   wild chicory, groundsel, hogweed, all specifics
of their stem-endings, the magic of nothing essential but echoes a softer
sound to meaning it there, provides (includes) their absence

Is giving onto something else, how embankments
embellish the paths, lastingly unapparent
as I already knew well

What does an apparition of meadow flowers
outlive if not declining visions?   they do
escape naturally but console a
certain 'and yet…'

A trace of strangeness more or less
shapeless, the trance of enigma

Frail kinds but a circulation beyond all
sign of breaking down, which the flowers
probably squander, at a world (hell)
of emergent surfaces

An invisible effacement opened
in these flowers, in desire as
long as a meadow walk

Note

I had been reading Philippe Jaccottet in French and English for many years, so was particularly moved to come across his last published poems in the version translated by John Taylor. I wondered whether I could work with these texts in their English form in some way and also add to it material from Jaccottet's earlier work. So, I have produced some reversionings drawn from translations by Ian Brinton, John Taylor and Mark Treharne (Mark first introduced me to Jaccottet).

Jaccottet himself was suspicious of over-elaboration, despite his own wonderful ear for rich concatenations of language, so there is something rather arrogant risked here, but I hope that as well as a tribute, this derived writing can be an intimate form of dialogue, even if at two removes. My title comes from his phrase 'avec un grésillement dans les éteules / comme d'étoiles à ras de terre' (*Last Book of Madrigals*, p. 52)

Sources

La Clarté Notre Dame and The Last Book of Madrigals, translated by John Taylor (2022)

Through an Orchard, translated, with an essay, by Mark Treharne (1978)

Jaccottet, translated by Ian Brinton (2016)

And, Nonetheless: Selected Prose & Poetry, 1990–2009, translated by John Taylor (2011)

Rainforests Apiece

Here plants grow on other plants, temperate than tropical, surfacing their 1 percent hope   enchanting relics have forgotten us, but not to exist

A damp arc is rainforest stretching west, fragments newly remoted, their invisibles a screen demoted

A remanent tree was rainforest until its own remnant offers a rainforest's sequel, its micro-return

Post-leaf verdant luminosity, fungus and leafmould in spate   epiphytes belabour the trees in non-parasitic scaffolding, however fragile (tinted) the root-clutch on thin upland

Heavily caked untossed crouch-world,
lichen whiskers vouch for lungs on trees

the furry aura many-footed
step by step   a spore
lodges in a knot-hole

rain begets outwash, begets
fungal clam and clamp, dampness
counter-sweeps the flow

in wilderness post-nature
is grovelled to its purest

Stems of deforestation plugged into rain ghettoes, terrestrial cramp is rainforest renewal

The only clues to renewal are already overgrown, how antique cover will green over the desert pleasances, the immediate sparse trees of always were

Pollen cores amid fossil precedence, the yearns of paradise a flattened clinging crowns the boulders, passable stunting towards the thin place, harsh crouch unadrift of the sacral

Hollow enough for a shrunken
nestling ghosts of the stood as
landscapes evacuate their trees
how secluded promontory
has its girdles, its oaks
stubbed against desert

Discontinuous blanket, now micro-oaklands drip mosses and lichens to coarsen the gap, rehang the rip a face of attenuation stalked (plugged) at its own rimlessness, this is the pulse of congealed rain, temperate turmoil

Dwarfed only by their persistence, a gully of delayed spikelets, inflates a mushroom zoom of compression

However boulder strewn
won't burst its saplings
these knuckles are vertical,
how they stunt (coalesce)
at their slowest shunting

How does apex emerge if not spread in drifts, raking across the very trunking of it? as fragment rainforest dares its own survivor species

Hidden worlds as carpeting a trash vegetation, reefs in trees gruesome chambers blister the surface

Spare paths of veteran trees coiling their abundance, the springs of any sprig retrenchment the wooded ravine conspires insignificance, respires the margin's vegetation of dedication

Plant-blind until seduced by a
new tininess of diversity
wizened to a corkscrew as
mosses ride out the trunking

temperate as unmapped,
imperceptible as a
smallest encapsulation

these relics their own
wreaths, unshaven by
damp or drizzle

Packets of fern-splay scatter a waiting lurk, tree-anchors arouse intimate secondaries, moss their unconditional hide

How radical microclimates pelt the gorges   steeply sloped to a hidden code, a portent per tamp of oak, how it might divert the grazing

A world of wound at sheepwrecked pastoral sheen, green edible desert's huge scope of a no across rewilding

Postindustrial rainforest recovers a site lime-maimed, this time without any need to wrestle the plantations

Sheep and grass their hill-shaven self-image, other natures will contrive to land again on a least of need

Wet woods (caked) in moss-locked bays of seclusion   stony ground allowed a return to its self-seeding profile, ripples of amassment cheat nibbled clearface

Intermixture of ferny trunks re-able the kneed trees, tufting the insistence, bittersweet the juniper alley assistance

In tight selection of disturbance prickly scrub is the latest fortification, rainforest no longer cowers at this rasping access

unloses rainforest at a fenced hip, resurges along the far side, exclosing
bids bilberry and bog asphodel remain   the verdigris sheen no longer
shed on sheep

When does a wedge (wrangle) of rainforest suit its own ledge?
assigned edge not so undersigned at first shaves of pasture, mature trees
lead their own betweens until browsing is in time with the tall lets of a
larger hoof, feels its way without gutting

Woodland displacement never simply a matter of tilt, foisted amplitude
has other sorrows: remainder trees heap their carapaces   sparse
hereafters of no such drag

Moss-descriptive sticks wrestle
the drying light but no such dying
now a steeper clasp betwigs

Twisted trees as boulder-strewn but foaming   boughs bearded and
sprouting not with their own, the lichen conduit   knot-holes until
they protect/project festoons, each fissure its own moon

Unlikely (perjured) growth serves
the underlying installation, roots
raid (cradle) the rocks

Dank saturated crowns oppose spearhead fir dark ranks, as in rain's
own counter-looming   penalty leafmould in the oceanic zones, what
ancient extractable oak pays for in outputs of pine

Atmospheric dust and tree leachings   feed the aerial keep of fern

Bones of landscape darkly unforbidden to pines casing, the yield-class
maximal

It takes latticework to glimmer a gentle smirr, just this crests the
horizon of the span, accidents of rainforest

Arching a sheen of wings, lichens touch neither earth nor sky, alive only for tree-current

Exposed oceanic ground rippling with unflayed sheep

Praying the contorted station, longest durance of a sapling's thronging, fabric given upon origin, its regeneration halo the true scrub

Eco-colonial invasion will retreat only at non-riddance of rainforest heartland,   the community spurt apart from no other domain, forest people

Vertiginous (gnarled) cladding,
woodrush and bilberry,
the felted scarp

natural ventures of
disturbance, bio-intricacy
was never woundless

A carbon-rich soil in high canopy, moss-humus   or seedbanks asleep on the forest floor under an alien blanket

Only a squatting tree can scan (unscar) its raw leafmould, crouch and wait at limb   relocal, re-admittances

Rainforests on their own unsown manoeuvres   fast viridians dripping closeness

Note

My main resource (though with no actual quotations) for this poem has been Guy Shrubsole's ground-breaking (or ground-healing) book *The Lost Rainforests of Britain*, 2022. The poem is dedicated to all those working to restore and enhance these crucial habitats.

In the Ring of Fresh Releases

after Gustaf Sobin

Translucently numb, dreaming a wordless   seed immanent flesh,
damp breath, the humus trolls it

A miracle reading the cloud, of matters in shadow   how earth ciphers
its meadow

Each increment the continuity of a tree, an elaboration of genesis

Acceleration secretes (swims) a not yet happened   velocity of perpetual
whisper

green mirror the agility
of green axe   earth shudders
its wrists   of wisdom,
thick probe

Charred claws (roots) alight on flakes of seed   tentacles otherwise the
studs of wound, immediate migrant hollows

Undulant water blows fibre, the spokes of spiralling greens   volutions
of ebullient cast

Silage a language residue pillages its origin magic   colossal isolation
breathes out its repression with the flesh of intent, proffers an existent
sigh, blossom in crystal

Plump somatic spirit, ragged resinous body, a blue earth swift as ash
muttering balance, limbs of thick liquid

Innocence flowering an inevitable in the throe of its spiralling, a
meadow's radiance violent enough to enter   raw threading of those
undeafening vestiges of the first enormity

something in me shreds
(the touch) a not mine   and so not
shatter the windflowers thicken

forever press rich spindles
with branches of gliding   sycamores
clamour a wider forever less,
how roots arose

An edge yields to its mesh, the mirage splinters *in* cage   how these
lunges flare a flesh stretched for prisms, landscape whiter than its thrash

Eventual each thing, a solitude is billowing seeds, the earth shivering
the elation   a cold dawn but free of its glassy fruit, as forever wider
than   soar the gathered, siphons the thirst of its breath vibration

Deepest into orchard, waiting for recurrent tissue, searching a clay for
the perching root   filament germinal enough as a return to coalescence
off detachable rock, entire iridescence of each finger

Perspective in breathing its eclipse, crouching for encagement
successive oscillations of rock, flint of an immaculate leap   magpies or
dragonflies scatter the hesitation

Pollen its own stutter furiously vertical   reverberates the bristling of
an oak, sprinkling on edge to an earth of clamps and squeezes   spawns
the eyes of green at a single step, crams the echoing

The least stones exhale their field, breathing a lip from a skin of
minerals, until it is mist which tastes the wind

A renaming forced to reply its cast, rubbing the dense echo is effigy,
issues in the mould of hidden trees   against the air's own illegible drift,
restitute and return, do not invert the path but refract the ride

bracelets but no darkening of
crystal, pitting a stem against its
tall transparency   scratches
(chrysalids) of effusion,
the slipped unravelling

Anatomy of the intervals that live their surface replies, fugitive alighting
to constitute a sacred   how it was saved unhappened, cleavage,
source, cloud

like bunched floating, what light
pulls the stone begs whiteness,
heart-skins, echoing walls

Rasped, not clotting rivers   listen to the glowing springs bunch over
ground,   ovals of it dense with orchard

What is it an intricate earth expiates, in protracted collapse, in pressure
of archaic increment?   a stuttered-entire body assumes fibrous spasms,
diminishing cubes coincide   the elements of rooted leaves wandering
their irretractable swarming: what clatters caresses, drawn inward

Curls of interval to thin the abyss, breath rotates the tongue   its gift
extravagates as flint in flickered shadow, the forehead receives suddenly
a reedy grain dusted off long scoopings from its milked body   a
dream of disk forces the eye to bend to its throat

Sudden terraces of leaf   in direction of but with no length of
vanishing, beneath an oak's sitting gift   spreads facetted, fingered
splinters

Halves of flesh stammering the lashes of a last field

Bleaching the risk of a single tremor, leaves lay matted but breasted
at their own murmur   bees on hand all morning, the space is nets
entering their own waves

A lime accelerates against the longer tails of ash   not plummeting to dissolve as light squirts white, scars are troughs of the same scars, a first tear

Ephemeral twinged wisp, an instant throbs a feather rushed, extinction simultaneous awesome relic   charred breath spindles its stirring in fixed wonder

Incrustations of tree jettisoned onto breath beneath the skin   cellular flesh meshing with a surface sheathing it erratic

this darker fire is painless,
ululating between lapse and reweld,
bone-sculpture of the process,
pulsate weave in warts of green

Under the earliest trees a field of conciliation, engendered ground in transit   like beads of the hill, like dawn a germinal dust, a peripheral confluence   the curve of meaning its breath between each instant

Intervals spend the night whispering a meadow   clashing thirsts cleanse themselves on silent surfaces   until dawn tilts the clay onto light, fleeces of containment talk up the density

Punctures the darkness from masking another needle   love alights beyond this ring of weightlessness, is branded (held mumbling) even deeper

Unwheeled, in clotted opening   lapidated light may chant it without realising, green syllables that dissolve in clay   lift each small equal lash to particles of orchard

rotate such weights into
their hole   in half-turns
of those opening oils

A wasp rots gold in orbits of intricate feather, autumn ignites the new hours of thunder   is weather's ear for a dusky blaze at the root of each (translucent) crackle of bloom full-fused

A weightless enveloping nudges chambers of wanted tissue, wheeling the chant across its ellipse

a space which the ear
heard moving, generating
a magnitude (ribbed)
of breath

Cleaves to its own ruptured (reclaiming) expanse   the rim a thrust on its syllables, the entity is saying space is the shred (named) in projections, the membrane blown against its own fibres

Accretion without withholding whatever lost reach its orchards replied: this its infinite quiver withstands

Note

This cento, or patchwork, is drawn from Gustaf Sobin's *Wind Chrysalid's Rattle* and is responding to a fascination with how he conjures from the sense of ephemeral effervescence or evaporation a mysterious solidity or crystallization out of the common elements (both floating and landing) of so many interpenetrating circuits, exact granules of remote tactile horizons.

Dunwich Birch

For Simon Collings

Or take the points of an arrow or rocket at the exhaustion of its power of ascent, or the line described by its fall, & we never dream of classing it with the segments of a leaf, in the latter instance the line of limit is altogether positive & energetic. —Coleridge, *Opus Maximum*, 305

A springiness of jolted tree, free stress
catapult off tendril, branch bounces
the absorbance, surplus insistence
given a cord of leaf

Tension at scrupulous kinship,
a coil never lunges except
to prod a storm

Strings of trees are nothing beside
their foils sprung across   no recoil
other than root a tail of drag

Coil sprung to a leaf-spray   tapered,
in the torsional reforms of compression

Storage of release as no violation
of original shape   its spiral of a spring:
open coil to nearest helical expression

What springs at birch are its
reels of reserve, all
unshafted except as it shifts
compression, its
lightest taut at sweep

As if sprung coil could also be
seepage, tidal turn on tendril

How do trees reach their release/rest position? Leaves pull in tensile parallels, root already fully extended (not vented) but held to a vertical pole

The growth retort springs compression,
repose along the next tension
unfolding, drawn
across veins of the sun

A birch-thwack of pioneer rest:
from birch thinness to forest edge,
any minimal drape will re-pose advance

Releases its own steadiness in a
para-release, questing the next
settlement off shoot

Elastic deformation is what the
birch pours to its store
of origin

At its typical close-coil
pitch, increases (extends) the
shelter-friction for all
of a wood's edge

Prayer's climax series itself sprung
unstooped   what plays core
was intense rotation-devotion,
compact scape ahead of drift

Its borne tussock flung to new clasps,
the spring initials of birch, apparent
screw-thread in lesser crush,
tendril awaits torque beyond twirling

Birch stretch no longer a blank
hutch, roots stanch the compression
they launch

A nested prefatory at plain jostle, seismic absorption at sky level attainment insists on rebound of pole   how birches flit root in their stride on station, then feed the vertical prolongation a bud at a time

This sluice of growth (emerges to sprung)
is its own counter-suction   convergence
along the release-thud, fresh loading

Enhance vertical slide (abides)
is the shiver expression of tree

Poles are rods towards uncontorted scope,
co-tensive at the pressure offer   prayer at its
unconditional additions of reversion,
its sprung ontology

A leaf's elastic a whole birch
concertinas for, smoother quake
off solar pull

How tooled bark is crimped at its climb,
every craning tree has this vibration,
broadening the rankle of ascent

Birch retouches internal persistence
at green stretch, resting at its farthest interval,
then decking it, ungaps its sprung-to

Springy birch continual relaunch less
revision, pumps the spiralling instability
through a bough-table, is whip at crest of rest

Arisen roof from which to sequence, carried at brunt, prayer's limbs from torque at the carried root, rests similars at its ipse endorsed   the otherwise of dormancy gives way to sprung husbandry of shoot

Strips of tree shape an
arc, will withstand clearance
uncrisping its small acre

How leaf in sprig keeps
contact at its followers:
torsion is terrain of branch
come to root, every portion
(in leaf) guides the
coil of trunk

Sessile invocation, from sills of root
bunching the flexible spokes taut,
veins select their surfaces

Like any previous accession of root it needs the lessons of the springy for
looming a lean profile or the entail of prayer as undiluted sweep of rest:
the reach of a given (undriven) compression

Expected tree cloak is slimmer
from sprung, tantamount to
scruples of root-creep

Rampant though unprolific reserve
in tension   horizon no longer self-
consuming at its stretch out life

Lurking woodland the beam of its
sprung-from   preserves impulse
at every fresh survival   tall wands
to relational brim

How does a sprung-with answer layers of cluster?   at prayer's veering
silence across the unthreshed enclaves

The sole underived release is onto limb:
truth as the nearest given-for
with primary compression, unstrategic
being, birch

Such springy configurations
at no extra rigging

Birch spring (become sprig)
is its customary range, stranger
than lunge   what is it a prolonged
jounce convenes?

How else to comfort a dent
in the light and then settle it
for a sway of limb?

A wave of leaf a load at
least holder wound through
root axle (helical access,
open-soil springing)

Spring-set tendril at low
solid height for greater
surge, resists un-
conical components

Any intimation of leap shed first
at ingrown spring, transfers pin joint
along flow of joint, no other fissures
than at crackle of leaf

How a birch seals its own release in relief of how what clings is still the opened future   each branch budding the cushioned punch of its bracing flare

Rootal soar puts all this padding
through the latest fetch of curve:
if decompression trounces
leaf it renounces no such trust among
ligaments of bobbing birch

Due Tree, True to Repair

What is it repairs a tree towards?   from which horizon reinstall integral
damage spared across site?

Restoration accordingly steps of branches once stopped   it doesn't take
tree-shatter to unspurn the healing, from stub to tip

Harmed beech is untouched until it repairs *to* its climate of immediates

Repair was the grounding initiation, pristine news of surface as proud
flesh encrusting branch

What is it trees repair if not their own unailing surrender?   as they
contend with jagged fragments (pittances) of an indifferent availing

What aches a tree's repair if not its transfer wound?

It trees the winding boughs until they restore (propel) their rifling
scrape of shoot

Injury has an unceasing trait in repair, for the tree of it to bid for
position, let be its replacements

As repaired object is defect unclenched, its failure too accessible for
defeat

Tree the plethora of vexed function, what repair taxes with more drastic
internal salves

No tree will reproach a healing tendency, lets repair approach   as from
the first to resume ungladed

To inhabit what it repairs of its middle ground, its co-extensive intervals

The immediate measure (continuum) is body weight not lacking the
burdens (jackings) of repair

Proliferates without being provided, until repair divides and assembles the throbbing, offers vertical tree its lease of thronging bed

Beech seeks a tempo of repair around its own one convergent blotch

The figure of repair surpassing any display of harm, emits touchables of the new concession, unpatched horizon

Repair to cruise new actuals, a tree for a spine, rattled leaves smooth its slipway

How reparation launches at tree as much as from it, healing is scar-transmission, every transition gutters a scoured trunk

Tree hulk fuels the repair-medium, infills a ceiling gaped at (uncapped) enough not to darken its own herbal dosages

Even a young tree's commonality   not pre-injury but reserve proportions of receptive grace

No withered measure to repair's immediacy, the trees are incontinent in absorbent scope, every breaching bough its own bandage

Tree repair in earliest foragings, skirmishes

Restoration at a far below any not yet become   plunged seed was its own pleading, at first contention is undifficult branch

Repair the figure of a tree that nearly was, damaged at/by intimacy of origin, salvaging the trials of gift

Less inherent interconnecteds than relations of (narrates with) peculiars of repair, mounts an incisive blade (swathe) prayer

Upstream (upleaf) not simply surviving injury but its endangered cue

Repair the unhidden rejoinder, how the longest bough might break before it, and circumvent any naked socket

Repair to add (contrive) a new sleeve for the opaqueness of these
violated givens, thicker than any branch is prone to

New (vertical) rigidities can flex (concede) how a tree grows taller from
initial shock

Repair *is* an expressive, not just cure of the stock   differentials of
branch skeleton went nothing awry

Allows, impels the part to inaugurate its versioning (nursed, creased) of
the whole

Came repair actual, completion across all the failed potentials of plant,
the lesser it is entirely able to be, or tree more than tree

Damage is a form of the future but never its norm   foundational harm
is not conclusive storm

Restore the resurrection of contour to its tree preliminaries

Transmutable reserve in tree, every fresh tendril is already a flesh rebuilt

No tree primal flow but explores its original becoming, at the wound let
come: dent as refuge diverting departure, anticipating resource   the
re-healed snag foaming at the congeal of symbol

Both these smarts (non-avoidances) begin in tree: seed and canopy

Progresses the real towards this undepleted shattering of tree: thorn or
shrub

Repair averts what streams off tree (crusts its traces) from exclusive
consolidation, here is no girth of unaided root

Amends from all available scarcities   abled tree from its own internal
shortage, until a tilth of tendril, its shareables

How tree repairs its own remainder of the prior, completeness less
integral than participating the substitutions   supplicatory instep,
arching its cratered cavities

Spare the tree, repair its stood

Inaugurates the recuperations of speculative growth, a leaf swathes
the air it is flurried by   tremors of relief whose micro-calluses resist
repulse

Its pioneer sprig already schooled to a reinstallation   at the margin
(tangent) between collapse and remission

Remedial treasures, to assume a forest on course, halt and reverse at any
new bare tree horizon, reparation in the bias (lesion) of tree-crash

A green leveller at forest fringe, fungoid allotment tree to tree, wound-
select, gouged erect

Assets (sap flow) injury-starved until each gash's irreducible register, a
new dribble of relief

Incision staking transfers, stress in trust of the new scabs of resilience,
full flesh of the violation

Exudation or secretion, how a fresh cradle-cap does encrust the crown,
bent leaf alert pustule, blister craters at oppositional (new-sealing)
borders

Tree flesh in advance of its own rescue-mesh, injects a final residue
frontier

Repair without reprieve, tree replete along its broken lines, the props of
oblivious held tissue   non-convulsive, need-free

Sustain an arena for lacerated (unpeeling) scum of the primal   encasing

A Plantness Verges its Planthoods

This piece of writing is a cento loosely derived from parts of Michael Marder's remarkable *Green Mass: the Ecological Theology of St. Hildegard of Bingen* (2021) though with some additional material of my own. Where Marder attempts a phenomenology of the verdant I am sketching more the variants of an ontology of the verdant, and in a spirit less adamantly post-metaphysical. I don't feel the greenness of green gives us quite that sort of temporality but I offer these versions in tribute to Marder's resourceful and daring explorations.

The plantness of this verge, is tree instilment, more than evenly renewal,
promises terrestrial fold, the greening prior to emergence

enchantment was first its sown de-tract, then a slotted plenitude at its
verdant retreat   decreation itself slopes (poses) green

intangible deforestation but a palpable speculative beginning not
running dry of its vegetal portion of the orbit   creation pervades its
own doubled meaning, verging the veering

greenness 'comes down' (salvation) to identify the seed, gives prior
blossom its own branching, redemption through-leafed

wind back from the falling fruit to greener sprouts giving the way of
reversible vegetal iteration, co-indicators of flowering path

green tenets not exhausted in accomplishment, a lucidity of graced matrix

brimming past desert at the make-sense (take-search) of branch surfaces,
a modality of horizon sprung from the verge   where re-enactment
bespeaks life outliving its force-norms, entities (divine) given common
confluence

green world to be at world newly become its gives-world, what was then
to be dashed past at the devoids of human existencing   incarnation
misses (nurses) its voice without this new (former) irreducible

we are those others the plants stray from, our own deforestation fiercely
the freshest at withering   a global manifestation infested with uproot

lodged on the edge of the narrows this plant-other we have succeeded to
between the else-entirely of slender twig or shoot

branch is mobile lift, enough to touch the terrestrial at its opposite
gravity, so to improvise its bird-hoist

an overarching already-not, a not-yet branching toward, the middle of
lack is its verdant patience, suavest sole point, no untainted linchpin

the shape of a tree that won't think itself but switches traces, a
premonition of outcome

universal scope of radicle non-suspension, tree's vertical subterranean,
the far cry of foliage

what is the threshold of the verge, where its verdant grass is grafted onto
the verticalities of sap or at a thrust of uninterrupted root?

but still coasting that transition   its material overstretch an elastic
immutable   akin to solid projection   plant pasts reiterate their
novel conforms

planthood neither fruit nor flower but converging each cardinal   a
tissue like this is not decay per se unless at its unhitching association
(branchless leaf)

no translational shortcut which is not saddled with a green issue

heaven as a small facsimile of the world but differently winged   what
hovering would be to a terrestrial fold, fading no more than greener

unassailable lapse reminisces unsubstitutable verge   subsequent re-
covery was no spectral replacement

intermaterial ligament voicing issue connectives, bonds of output
culled betweens from the corners of among

in means partaking spirit, a trans-species throng telling it to the stitches,
all the preamble of occasioning rootstock

a vigorous witness stranded on (lent) both sides, migrates the gathering
kinetic offering for the two-pronged replay of soul

attunement its own unintended surplus, but not through the effects of
adjustment

soul reinserts its constellation, as a quasi-imperfect notation, the rhythm
of resonance

devastation is no distortion of resurgence, implants its veil of sighs and
tears

fainter vibrations of silence to efface the void, co-vibrations of root
abiding (not shivering) leaf

the symphony of existence at its scarce adjunct, a silence foisted on a
disposition of plant

greening green full to its outer envelope, so that it might be situated
right at the swathing

that giving standpoint is at the middle of its sending, a missive
brimming through all the brackets of plant

greening the green bristling with reception   as a root is already
written (ramifies) onto branch

jagged eternity at a floridity of horizon, how it is to offer what every tree
result does permeate

as plant is a meantime beside itself, the indwelling (wrapped so) bridging edges, transmission of what nestles (defaults to) another intimacy than itself

a cycle ensconced between seed and seed, sieves the preview of adjacent arising   attributes are linear vegetal but rotating on horizonal sheath

an excess within but modestly refreshes world at its manifest greener: discreet initials of creation   how the fruit of a plant's thinking pre-takes

the non-relational gateway that stays to express an interwoven witness, forging a plant medium

in the beginning suspension of not yet beginning again, a mystery harking back beyond the in-between at its unique creases of inception

clusters of finitude at once too rebegun to be the sole in-finite   greening the green will not be stripped to its own threshold, will replenish the disposition of horizon

a tree visible to the waters of existence, how its reflections dovetail with seeings akin, aqueous dawn

kiss green depths off the surfaces of humankind, the one intimacy without edifice it will house

leaves kiss sunlight across the threshold of a filter, wings of plants are the mouths of butterflies   plant-knowing in the wisdom of this interior brush

a reflux of plant spanning (inflecting, adumbrating) soils of the sky, a tree-mouth lipped at its root

green mass digests its competing models to kiss a hinge of faith at its lightest mediation: nourishes horizon

no longer obsess so many counter-stiffnesses   sense the sharper
immutables of green, its vertical patience

Weep the Tree

Weep the tree, a tree wells up
its unexchangeable station   wipes any
runnel-dread from roots

How trees weep is tangible law,
swerveless branch crescent,
curve overworking any descent

Weep a tree for the keeping
of its symmetrical tilts   its
vaulting cavern in roofless tension

Not stiff in weeping but compaction at the drooping immediacy   swathes of cultivar singleness, scans each redrawn (fully mourned) droplet for drape

What weeping seeps into
doesn't protrude, simply induces
a broader sopping up

A slant origin of standing world disclosed through spread (unbedded) weeping,   the earth's buckling tide draws back too far for reversion to root   the shelter is tall enough, unconditional housing where horizon edges the grief of it

What nearer than weeping boughs
intend?   how they siphon their
arteries of attention

The chaplet of inwoven leaf is a weeping template, along off-stem seedless beads, their downward assignation

Gravity curvature an incitement
to saturated pleading, re-signs the
billowing   accepts its grief of

architecture, designated default

Weep the tree off its rigid limbs, incline it fuller than it can taper   no heed to drape the earth at this streamy overhang   the downtilt has its own planetary curve, horizon's easing bough

Not a twig cricked but a bowed branch
weeps its retention, the mitigating droop
of entire disposition

Less return off shoot than resting in concession, the mournable elbow of arcade   where both together switch through root to vault, declare the apex of weeping-from

Curtains of sagging leaf sweep the ground
yet can't create a mound, weep their
own skimmed trail

Harmable, yes, but not to be
degraded more than their own
droop

Even where a branch slouches
it is not limping through

Any branch can be brought to weep,
just one deviant co-exploring cell,
slight sunlight of the aberration

Every non-weeping tree is beset with
its own unshaggy skyward, primordial
wrapping does otherwise

The toys of upward growth or
an unbraced arch earthward

Slime flux for invisible wounds, what
weeps a condition of tree, the secret
of what trembles oozing

Token limbs drop no sap, authentic
drooping left nothing to sip

Cultivar trees at a weeping
for unwooded world

Are the aberrant cells themselves sighs of rejoinder, offering the earth its own least incorporation?   weeping its wildings so conjured to shape, not injured

Tree lamenting the instinct of
its clusters   is this crouch-crown
so weathered from below?

How to mourn the trees' stricken
(uncorroded) height as against
their own counter-formed
lament?

Are they ducking (or sniping)
the eroded atmosphere, its
unassuageable entourage?

Wept the unplayable advantage
of bare ground

As the trees wail their congruous
distortion, such shrouds
of reapportioning

Weeps the tree of its terrain, the deflated
saturation   how sorrow is
plant as rescuer, ascribing
(foliating)
the grief

A willowy slant that never disrobes,
undulating soil can't match
this fountainous arcade

Weeping a broadleaf cascade,
untoppling the surrender

To weep a tree is to relieve the grief
it diverts from pinnacle, delving into
the solitudes of its petition

Stare into the manner of its mourning,
share the inter-teeming   a tear stoup
at the knelt of leaf

Willow, hazel, cedar, cypress, maple, spruce, birch, fig, mulberry at the weep-towards, sprinkle solace over all a plant re members

www.ingramcontent.com/pod-product-compliance
Lightning Source LLC
Chambersburg PA
CBHW031637160426
43196CB00006B/457
* 9 7 8 1 8 4 8 6 1 9 7 3 9 *